Behind the Frontline

Alana Jones

BEHIND THE FRONTLINE

First Edition

MAGORIA BOOKS
Toronto, 2019

This book is dedicated to my family,
whose unwavering support can never be measured:

Jael, Danuvi Zoli, Adel, Veronica, mentors, friends

To all the committed, social justice driven workers on the
Frontline in the nonprofit sector, showing up daily to
positively transform the lives of marginalized
individuals.

To your respective families who understood your
determination and provided you with the unapologetic
permission to work in the trenches of this beautiful city
called Toronto.

This is a work of fiction.

Names, characters, businesses, places, events, locales, and incidents are either the products of the author's imagination or used in a fictitious manner.

Any resemblance to actual persons, living or dead, or actual events is purely coincidental.

CONTENTS

Preface

In my practice, community work has led me to seek higher education in the field. It has provided me with an understanding of social justice and client focused advocacy with an emphasis on successful outcomes determined by those whom I support. The paths travelled through marginalized communities allowed for careful examination of their individualized stories and journey to healing, recovery, metamorphosis and self-discovery.

Personally, as a child I had an understanding of homelessness. In my culture, the word homeless was not part of our national narrative. Homelessness became part of my Canadian vocabulary. The words I heard and used before were: Wayward, Destitute, Vagrant, Vagabond, and Displaced. Each word represented a different subsection of the community. Wayward was associated with youths who left home to be on the streets with friends. Destitutes were used for those who became overwhelmed with the trials of life and family and sought solace on the streets or in local hospitals. Vagrants and Vagabonds were the names used for those who looked really untidy and unwell, mentally disturbed, drug and alcohol dependant, while Displaced individuals referred to the many men and women abandoned by their families due to violence, poverty, family separation and migration.

I recall at the age of ten, my seventeen year old brother making the decision to leave home without any plan of where he would live because he felt my mom had too many rules. Armed with a packed knapsack, with un-filled dreams and hopes that any young man should have, he left home on a warm Sunday morning in February. He would return for food when the streets became rough, and upon his return my mother would attempt to give him another chance of success. This was oftentimes short lived as he never returned to living in a 'home'. Instead, he roamed the streets for another six years, contracting HIV in the process. He spent the last 2 years of his life in and out of the hospital before his death at the lucrative age of twenty five. His story, like many of the homeless men and women I worked with, informed my practice of intersectionality and individuality.

The focus of my work remains grounded in individ-ualized approaches unique to one and necessary for all, and a continued purpose to improve the outcomes of indi-viduals marginalized due to physical and mental health, addictions, poverty, gender, socio-economic status, immi-gration status, identity and religious belief.

Each year, the stories gathered from unique individ-uals have created a fabric of knowledge with colours of pride, isolation, injustices, advocacy, renewed spirit, re-silience. These stories are our triumphs and challenges, their history and herstory, and more importantly; our lived experience. A path travelled.

This collection of stories and fictional characters are an intersection of a writer's dream and a social advocacy world in collision. It provides a backdrop to frontline work and a fore front to clients. In addition to the mu-tual treasures they carry within and share in a desperate attempt to get help that's filled with empathy and not sympathy. It also serves to support, while steeped in social justice work amid emotional and mental violence.

Treatment based approaches that are not always repre-
sentative of beliefs, customs and identity, culture and
heritage are ever so present.

*"Their yesterday became my tomorrow, and their tomorrow
became my yesterday"*

Alana Jones

Foreword
by Nancy N. Mayer

Behind the Frontline gives the public a glimpse at the complexities that frontline workers such as housing workers and other social service workers face while working with homeless people. Workers are drawn to this work for many reasons, but the most common is a fervent desire to help. Few are prepared for the toll on their own mental health and how it will change their view of the world. The needs are great and the services are scarce.

Like soldiers on a battlefield, they face an onslaught of psychological and physical violence with inadequate training and tools. Poverty, trauma, addictions, mental health and physical health issues leave people feeling sad and angry.

Inadequate housing that puts too many hungry, tired and hurting people in too small a space further traumatizes people who are already teetering on the edge. Society does its best to turn a blind eye to the root causes of homelessness and instead provides band-aids for cavernous wounds.

Workers must bear witness to those who will die and those who can't be helped. These preventable losses of human life temper the feeling of success when people manage to leave the life on the street. Those who do this work are seldom considered heroes; most are underpaid, under-resourced and under-appreciated. They come and go in this industry, seldom noticed for the real human sacrifices they make. One resigns and another is hired. Almost as faceless as those they serve.

This important piece of work puts names and faces to those who work in the shelter system. It highlights their struggles and invites the reader to see them, and those they try to serve and help. While facing almost insurmountable odds, these workers support the resiliency of the human spirit and some clients manage to transcend their circumstances. However, no one leaves the streets unscathed- neither those souls who live on the streets and in our country's shelters nor those brave souls who work to help them. This book tells their story.

Nancy N. Mayer, MSW, RSW

Foreword
by Gautam Mukherjee

I was privileged to work with Alana Jones for several years and saw first hand how she understands the Housing First model in a fundamental way. She seeks, and pushes others to understand the uniqueness of each person's situation while being single-minded in pursuing housing as the remedy to homelessness.

In the time we worked together, Alana experienced a number of significant personal events but was able to manage a large program and support her team to do excellent work in supporting people to permanently end their homelessness.

As a Trinidadian Canadian Community Practitioner, Educator and mother, Alana ensures she is never defined by the stereotypes associated with her unique identity and experience of becoming a manager at a young age. Given her professional and personal context, it is no surprise that Alana would focus her writing on the complex challenges faced both by people experiencing homelessness and by people providing services.

In Toronto, the work of supporting people experiencing homelessness can at times take on a feeling of absurdity. There are very few decent, vacant apartments, and the rents are out of reach. Even when clients have additional financial support to help overcome the financial barrier, they face discrimination from many landlords.

Sometimes, as seen in Justice Brand's story, workers find themselves trying to convince clients to try to find housing. Richie's story includes the sometimes-disastrous consequences of programmatic pressure to get clients into housing.

As with all battles, workers and clients on the frontlines of homelessness in Toronto are dealing with a system, and decisions made by others far away trying to come up with complex solutions. However, those in power assert that the simple solution of ensuring everyone has enough money for rent is very impossible to implement. Needing to deal with these absurdities and to cope with—rather than being empowered to smash—tremendous systemic barriers, contribute significantly to the stress and risks of burnout and vicarious trauma that workers in the system face.

All the best housing workers fight on many fronts—they fight daily for clients and they fight against the unjust systems which cause homelessness. They appropriately recognize that no one should be homeless and they work to make an immediate difference to those experiencing homelessness, while also acknowledging that it should be easier, and the housing solutions should be better.

The range of stories in *Behind the Frontlines* represent the range of battles that people experiencing homelessness and the workers trying to help people leave homelessness face.

Gautam Mukherjee
Executive Director
Mainstay Housing

INTRODUCTION

The last few years we have seen those working with homeless individuals sound the warning bells of a looming crisis. North American and European cities are facing a rise in the homeless population. Many attribute the increase to the economic downturn of 2009, while others argue that the constant migration and immigration are contributing factors. Today, the homeless population continue to grow as the gap between rich and poor widens. Twenty eight thousand and five hundred (28,500) individuals experience homelessness on any given night across Canada.

Frontline workers range from Mental Health and Justice Workers, Housing Workers, Follow-Up Support Workers, Shelter Workers, Kitchen Staff, Legal Clerks, Gerontologist, Volunteer Trustees, PSWs, Community Development Workers, Nurses, Addiction Counselors, Friendly Visitors, Child and Youth Workers to Disability Support Staff, ASL and Language Interpreters, Discharge Planners, Peer Workers, Food Security Advocates. The titles and roles are endless.

The commitment, dedication and sacrifice of these workers are immeasurable. Their roles are complex and layered. On a daily basis, they are driven with compassion and human spirit to improve the lives of the communities they serve.

Meet some of the faces on the frontlines, helping homeless individuals to connect to essential services and to secure affordable housing.

LUIGI

I came forward to share my story because the voices of workers are seldom heard. I was 24 years old when I decided to become a front line worker. I come from the average Canadian Italian family having no interaction with poverty or homelessness. I would say my immigrant family was living the 'Canadian Dream'.

After working as a financial advisor at a financial institution, I was ready to give real meaning to my life. Life in the bank was becoming increasingly difficult. I experienced two armed robberies and became anxious, anticipating the third. I requested a transfer to Retirement Planning. However, this change did little to calm my anxiety.

During my lunch break, I overheard a coworker sharing her experiences volunteering at a men's mental health facility. I was intrigued by the opportunity to support marginalized individuals and felt the sense of fulfillment she was experiencing. This conversation would become my seedlings of hope and introduction to the nonprofit sector.

She expressed how rewarding it was to give back and make a difference, and I somehow gravitated to the idea of giving back and making a difference. I had no intention to experience another armed robbery, so when my coworker said they were looking for volunteers who were interested in becoming a social service worker, I jumped at the opportunity. Three of my banking colleagues resigned within a week of each other and started working in various social service agencies. We were certain that we would be making a difference in the lives of the people we served. In retrospect, we were leaving one frontline position for another.

For six months, we learned the language of the social service sector. We became confident in providing life skills training, budgeting- which we excelled in as this was a real transferable skill, and informal counselling to grocery shopping. We enjoyed the rewarding work. As time went by, we were offered many training opportunities and was even offered contract jobs.

The impact on frontline workers as a result of increased homelessness and the opioid crisis has been tremendous. I want the public to know that homeless clients were dying in large numbers before the opioid crisis was called. The defining moment for the opioid crisis came when someone's son and daughter not fitting the homeless, impoverished criteria died. The City and Provincial officials now determined a crisis was at hand. Workers were sounding the alarm for a long time.

Currently, agencies have found a loophole to somehow articulate the exposure to "aggressive and unpredictable behaviors" as part of the job. Speculations. This disclaimer prevents frontline workers from stepping forward and talking about the impact of this environment. It's part of our job!!

Trying to seek support having re-read my job description, I recognized that by default, I had signed up for ongoing exposure to crisis, verbal, emotional and physical abuse. The revelation was crippling; one that would later determine the length of time it took for me to find the courage to access the support I desperately needed.

As my career progressed, working solely with men with mental issues presented many challenges, therefore I decided to work with another agency whose focus was broader and included youth homelessness. This would be my first encounter with the issues related to homelessness and vicarious trauma.

My banking colleagues and I supported each other, despite working with different non-profit organizations across the city of Toronto, in addition to the Employment Assistance Program (EAP) offered at our respective workplaces. EAP supports staff to access telephone counselling and in person counselling. However, the onus is left to the staff to connect themselves to these options. It's hard to access support when you are in denial of the impact; fearful to admit you are no longer mentally and emotionally stable to do your job.

I was always amazed at how many homeless individuals were in the city of Toronto. Some were hidden no doubt and considered a shame to this Toronto "the good" by city staffers. It's an opinion well hidden and one they would never admit.

No amount of training prepared me to experience the complexities of clients' traumatic stories and the systematic web of social services, addictions, poor mental health and abject poverty that I came face to face with daily.

In my fifth year as a social service worker, I experienced an all too familiar feeling. It was as if I was preparing for another bank robbery, except this time, there was no robbery. I was in fact getting ready for a job I had found very rewarding. Standing in the hallways of my sunlit apartment on January 12th, 2015, I finally admitted to myself, I NEEDED professional help.

I was afraid to share my experience with anyone. I was experiencing flashbacks from my time at the bank and was uncertain why this was happening. The complexities of my clients were tangible. It was more than the abuse; it was the lack of resources required for their unique needs, and the high caseloads impeded meaningful progress. The evidence was clear. We needed more affordable housing and wrap around supports to keep people housed. Not being able to find suitable housing options for my clients had taken a toll on my mental health. How does one keep showing up for work, knowing they are unable to adequately provide what the client is seeking? By the time I got to my doctor, I was unable to be at work after 3 hours without being nauseated. There were days I wished I owned a large housing complex to place all my clients and take them out of the cycle of homelessness.

Today, I no longer work as a housing advocate as I am now homeless after being unable to work and qualify for long term disability support. I currently live in a shelter just outside of Toronto's downtown core to avoid coming into contact with my old clients and coworkers. Hopefully in the next three months, I would have secured housing and regained stability. I would like to return to my old workplace and share the challenges frontline workers face, and how organizations can support staff more effectively. There needs to be education for clients too. No one wants to admit that, but clients must understand how their abusive language/ actions impact workers. Our job is to support, not to be exposed to ongoing acts of violence.

I wonder what's the percentage of client on worker violence in the city of Toronto and surrounding areas? No one tracks those!

The client is always right.

Housing is a right! No matter what.

We have to get the job done!

And I did…

JB

Former Social Worker
Currently Homeless at the Lakeshore

Justice Brand is the name. Call me JB for short.

Sitting here at this coffee shop waiting for my worker is a regular occurance. Today, I am going to determine how he can help me get ready for the winter. I live in a warm encampment on the Lakeshore. I have food and water; lights come from the highway. No meds though. Water I have. Did I say that already? I am not homeless but can certainly relate. Workers repeatedly ask for my address and my response does not change. The postman will bring my mails for me!! The postman not only knows my address; he brings me a treat with each delivery.

Like most who meet me, you are wondering what does JB stand for?

JB stands for Justice Brand. My parents wanted to make a statement. Who calls their son such a name? It's cool. Don't you think? Names with meaning always interest me. It tells a story. A story of people and from where they came.

There is no science to it really. Civil action is not a choice, it's a right. Voting is a choice I feel, although I know being a resident and citizen of a country allows you to vote. Bringing awareness about poverty, mental health and addictions are too visible to deny. It's the right of citizens to highlight the ills of society and do something about it.

Workers are out there running around trying to convince me that I need to live indoors; is that going to help me? They are trying to convince me to live the way they want, or the way society thinks I should. Why should I believe that they would not abandon the cause just like most people do? Workers go into deep thought when I ask them what makes them different. They all hope to make a difference. Two separate issues if you ask me. Some don't even know what motivates them beyond a pay cheque. What makes them different from all the bureaucrats?

"Safe and affordable housing is not a choice, it's a right regardless of who you are. I believe everyone has the right to housing regardless of gender, class, race or economic status." This is their scripted response.

Workers were taught well in school, they know all the

terms. I know them too. I use to be a social worker. Told people what they needed, how they felt, what medication was good for them, what they should eat, when to be outside, what was best for them and why they needed a therapist.

"Thanks for sharing." Another scripted response.

I said that too! No one cares where I came from and the struggles and sacrifices made for me to become Canadian. Lost my identity. The fighting in Bosnia, land of my birth was complicated and bloody, so my family fled here. Justice Brand is my real name. I hate the name my parents were told I should have. Who cares? The sounds of fighter jets never stopped in my head. My parents were rebels with a cause. They fought for education for all, the right for girls to be in school, the right for women to work outside the home. Here in Canada, they are nobody. We ran from fear and live in fear here. We never won the real fight for the people.

My parents would have loved to hear my vivid recollection of our journey, their determination, except they are afraid to come out side, but maybe you can call them yourself and say that I am doing well. I have failed them. I did not carry on their legacy. I came to Canada and instead of rising, I fell. Maybe I am not Canadian.

I have failed. I am not Canadian? Besides, how does a former worker access services where they sent their clients? The shame to see my clients in the same space I referred them.

And yeah we can meet but not here.

Maybe at the your office.

ZAIN

Mental Health and Justice Worker

I am Zain, a recent migrant from the Caribbean. My path to homelessness is an interesting one. I was encouraged to participate in a focus group that engaged residents around issues related to homelessness, youth violence and an aging population in 2016. At the focus group, the counsellor started by saying he wanted to hear from constituents/ residents about concerns they had regarding these issues and sought input to identify the gaps and identify areas of improvement.

Being new to the country and my Parkside neighborhood, meant I had limited insight, as I just was too new to make such observations and or suggestions. Nonetheless, I was eager to learn from my fellow residents, and so became my journey into community mobilizing and eventually becoming a Mental Health and Justice worker. I worked with a community agency that possessed strong restorative justice practices, and having a degree in Psychology helped me to quickly transition into this role.

The winter of 2017 came and there were several sleeping centers opened in the City of Toronto. It was the City of Toronto's response to bring the homeless and most vulnerable inside from the cold. There was much debate about the best response to the brutal Canadian winter. However, from my perspective, there appeared to be no clear operational plan in place to open these sites. It was indeed an emotional response from John Public.

Old Saint Nick tapped on the hearts of many Torontonians who daily would hop, skip, jump and avoid the said homeless individuals on their hustle to and from school and work. Once Christmas was over, all those passionate voices of concerned citizens disappeared. On one of my shifts, I was surprised to see how many youths presented at the Sleeping Centre to access service. No family members came looking for them. I was confronted with a reality I have never known or witnessed. How could this possibly be ok?

In the past, I had worked with women who had active involvement with the justice system. I understood they needed to be in a supervised environment as their family members were often the victims, but the Sleeping Centre was different. They came in hungry, cold, tired and often not properly dressed for the brutal winter. They were the clients that were barred from many other locations due to aggressive behaviors. They were individuals who were new to the shelter system, having opted to live outdoors under bridges, in their cars and encampments. This experience was very challenging for me. The chaos was beyond my understanding. Where did all these people come from?

Justifying the need for this new response to homelessness in the City of Toronto, local politicians indicated in their various news conferences that the spike being experienced by city shelters were from increased illegal border crossing. They argued this new phenomenon had stretched an already burdened system. However, as I completed intake after intake, for every 30 intakes in a week, there were one to three newcomers. The statistical picture painted in the news was untrue and exaggerated, but the public sucked it up.

The clients were abusive to staff and if ever we reacted we were disciplined. Management failed to address the complex needs of the clients, and our capacity to address the needs of the homeless was limited. We needed more specialized services onsite.

Clients were demanding and some even requested supports the programs were not funded to provide. I really tried to be patient but the abuse was too much. I do not want to paint a picture that all homeless and impoverished client as aggressive. In fact, many used the supports they were presented with and moved into shared housing or other housing options. Some even returned to family members.

Reflecting on my work in the last two years, I remain passionate about it and I want to keep working with the homeless, but that experience made me realize I wanted to focus on working with youths in a smaller setting. Here, I can provide more meaningful, long -term intensive case management. The staff to client ratio is often 1 to 30. It's not sustainable even if you found housing for all or supported many to return to their previous homes with family etc. Clients need follow up support and this is what I want to focus my efforts on.

As an immigrant, I am saddened by the level of poverty and lack of family involvement with the homeless population. A reality that is quite new to me. Where are the moms, dads, siblings and extended family? It takes a village to raise a child. The least they could do is help them get back on their feet. Too many broken families in Canada.

CLERIC

Yesterday I decided to seek counselling and maybe housing support. Now, don't get me wrong. I am housed. I want to know my options. My appointment is today around 2pm, if the worker even shows up. They can't even say my name correctly when I spoke to the receptionist on the phone. By the way, don't mispronounce my name either. *Clear ric*—Cleric. Say it, it's not that difficult.

I am who they call a social housing customer. I never understand who started calling clients customers. We are not choosing to live in substandard conditions across Toronto . Nice to meet you by the way.

Every time I venture into these social service agencies, I do my research, but these workers like to insult my intelligence and provide this long overview as if they don't realize "customers" read reviews. I read the profile of the agency and I know I am not on the streets but I am homeless and I am aware I don't have a formal mental health diagnosis, but what's the big deal. Many singers don't have a great voice, but they fill the biggest domes, festival stages and halls here in Toronto.

Anyways, I live with my family but I don't feel I belong there. Where should I really start? Let's start with the social workers script.

"Our program provides individual and family counselling, income support advocacy, support to homeless individuals, eviction prevention, access to harm reduction supplies and peer training. We work with clients to resolve conflicts with their landlords and support landlords resolve conflicts they may have with tenants around nonpayment of rent, guest traffic, etc."

Sounds like all they focus on is helping the landlord who oppress customers daily with the steep rents and no pest control. Yes landlords are needed to house people, but who tells the landlords how to be better in their role of supporting customers like me, who are totally dependent on them for a roof over their heads?

At the end of the day, my mom does not want to talk about me being a gay black man. She doesn't realize her lack of conversation around this issue is weighing on my mind. When I am with my family they speak as if I am not there. They take my money when I work part time at the library. I am depressed. Many nights I don't sleep at home.

Before I could complete my sentence, my worker interjects that I am fleeing financial and emotional violence. What is the point? Do they not listen? I thought they were suppose to listen and never forget that the customer is always right. I am not fleeing abuse. Violence can take many forms, and I recognize this but God is taking me through trials to make me strong and he is using my family to get the job done. When I am with my friends, I am the life of the party, I make people laugh when I go to Church Street. I never had a relationship because no one wants to live in a closet with me.

You have to understand my mom takes care of me. She cooks great food and she loves me. She makes sure I eat. You know my mother is ashamed of me? She is ashamed of having a gay child. All the neighbours tell her, "Maudy, your belly must be curse." My family looks at me with disgust. They love me still though, at least I try to convince myself. Truth is, it hurts to love them back.

What I notice working with social workers is that they love to use all these labels and then ask customers to think outside the box. Which box? The one they placed me in or the one they labelled, placed next to me without giving me hope? I concur, often the abuser is someone we love and trust, but I am not abused. This is my mom and family. They will never harm me.

My mom says that I have a spirit on me. She feels that when I get upset about the way I am being treated, I am not being myself, that I am another person. I use to work for the province and left my job. Not sure why. I just did. At home, I have a lock for my room, but each time someone goes in and changes the time on my clock.

They even change the radio to another station. Do you think I am crazy? My mom thinks I am. Dad said if I got more locks, the house would be safe.

What I need you to address is the pain and music in my head. I am ready for work. I need to be at Ottawa to plan the mission and protect my comrades. I need to book the flight for tomorrow. My dad says that I can do anything I want. He gave me research and details to complete the mission. I told him I was tired but he said get it done now. Let me introduce you to my dad. He is at home. His ashes sits on the dresser to the left of the room and when he wants to talk, he comes out and sits on the bed. He is quite impatient.

I am not fleeing abuse; I am living in it.

Besides, I can find a place on my own. I have a lot of credit coupons from the grocery and department store.

I have thought about returning to work and my mom says that she can provide me with counsel if I really need it. She is an educated woman. She said the neighbor can help me too. It takes a village to raise a child.

Eventually, I would hope a social worker helps me with reconnecting with my wife, daughter and grandchildren. I have not seen them in two years and I miss them. I may have said too much and mom won't be happy so I should stop talking.

SISTER MADELINE

Community Nurse and Church Chaplin

My name is Sis Madeline. I am a Chaplain at an inner city church in Toronto. My work on the frontlines with homeless individuals happened by chance. It really did.

In my previous role as a nurse Practitioner in the Township of Dawn, a rural community in Ontario, I seldom interacted with someone experiencing homelessness. However, as a Chaplain in the downtown core, the homeless population is very visible.

On the steps of the church, there is always about 6-10 homeless individuals congregating as I enter for mass daily.

The congregation brought this ongoing concern to the Bishop and a decision was made to create an area in the church basement to better support the needs of these individuals instead of ignoring their existence. This was a new concept for the church, but we felt a strong desire to make a meaningful difference.

There has been a myriad of things contributing to the homelessness crisis. I would say the actions of the church placed me at the forefront of the homeless crisis.

St John's Cathedral is the first religious organization funded to provide "Out of the Cold" services in Toronto. While we have gotten great support from other agencies over the years, they often say disparaging remarks about our religious beliefs. The church plays a pivotal role in the reduction or eradication of homelessness. We are more than soup kitchens. I want my frontline peers to know that religious proselytization is not part of our homeless outreach work. The church supports individuals who seek our assistance to exit the homeless cycle. We are first responders without the title.

When participants seek spiritual support, we will respond. This work cannot be from a holistic place if we are not addressing one's spiritual identity. This work transcends beyond religion. I'm not a social worker, but I'm moved to this societal crisis with heart, mercy and kindness. I often say to registered social work and social service workers, I walked to the frontline; irregardless of how I came, I'm here and doing the work.

SAL

Two Spirited Social Worker

Miigwech.

I'm humbled and moved by where we are all coming from to do this incredible work.

My name is Sal and I'm a two spirited.

I've been involved in the homeless movement from birth I would say.

Born on a reserve in southern Alberta where many resources are limited and my community is always struggling.

Access to clean, drinkable water, adequate housing and sustainable options for our overall growth have contributed to me feeling permanently homeless.

I'm often referred to as a "mixed breed".

I'm born to a mixed mom and Metis dad.

At least that's what I've been told.

I was left in the care of my grandparents from three months old.

I'm lucky not to be a part of the sixties scoop; my siblings not so lucky.

After high school, I hitched my way across Canada, finally settling in Brandon, Manitoba for a few years. I became restless again and made the eastern journey to Toronto.

I experienced homelessness as an adult for three years and decided I wanted to make a difference by becoming a social worker.

The strong presence of religious organizations in the fight against homelessness is profound, but it's a harsh reminder for me of the colonization and the negative impacts on marginalized groups and Indigenous communities. I am aware how religious organizations play a significant role. However, many try to force their beliefs on the clients accessing services from their church. Some religious organizations even have workers sign an oath as a believer.

Building trust is such an important aspect of this work, and during my career, clients have shared their stories of despair and triumph with me. From addiction and family breakdown to mental health, intellectual disabilities and loss of employment. There was so much gut wrenching stories, some replicating my own.

A significant number of clients have broken the cycle of homelessness. Those nuggets of success take me through the rough days. I'm yet to meet a homeless individual who enjoys living in the shelters. As shelter workers, we do our best to support clients, but conflict is always present. Varied personalities and experiences coupled together with confined spaces with rules, offensive odors, noise, violence and conflicting expectations are the perfect recipe for chaos.

Lived experience has shaped my ability to connect with everyone I work with.

It gives me a different perspective. With it though, are the invisible lines of boundaries.

The friends I've made as a homeless individual often don't understand or respect my role as a social worker. In their eyes, I'm seen as another authoritative figure telling them what choices to make.

I'm governed by rules and ethics.

I've lost great friends along the way.

I keep going.

Daily, I still see them and I think of ways to help them beat the streets. Many would never beat the streets!

Housing is expensive, addiction is real and the justice system won't always cut you a slack. Trauma associated with living on the streets is worse than a car accident I think. Beating the streets then seem like a joke.

Each year, I travel to a National Conference and I grapple with the conference costs. Can we dedicate some of those funds to securing an apartment for someone experiencing homelessness? The conference is committed to bringing communities together to share the work we have done. Not sure when we return to our communities, we share the knowledge. How do we prove that? Is there a demonstration of shared knowledge and cross training?

Their vision is incredible and it gives a platform for the issues of homelessness to be placed on the forefront of the cities we travel. The aim is to make governments accountable for a well-functioning Housing Strategy in Canada.

I'm currently a Transitional Housing Supervisor looking for partnerships to move the residents into permanent housing. It does not need to be dedicated to my community. I want to collaborate and see homelessness addressed for all. I feel specialized housing still creates gaps for individuals like me whose identity is complex and layered.

At the age of 45, I'm looking forward to retirement and reflecting on the last 23 years of frontline work. As an elder, I have much to offer young workers; at least that's what I think.

XANDAE

Xandae–pronounced Zanday
Former Housing Advocate Worker
Current Social Policy Developer with the Municipality of
Barrie

"The impact of front line work is yet to be told with authenticity. The successes we have with our clients are what we see on the subway ads and the annual reports."

The sacrifices workers make to deliver these success stories are yet to be told. I must disclose that I am no longer active on the frontline, given my new position as a Social Policy Developer with the Municipality of Barrie.

I became involved in the homeless movement through my constituency office. They were looking for part time workers willing to work with homeless men and women as it started to become a concern in the riding.

The work was exciting.

You have to take care of yourself.

Take time to exercise and eat healthy.

Talk to a therapist about the stress of the work.

Get support.

Be gentle with yourself.

I loved being outdoors and the clients I met came from all walks of life. This was back in 2000, when basement apartments were about $500. Apartments were easy to find and landlords' only request was for rents to be paid on time. Being a recipient of Ontario Works and Ontario Disability Supports Program was not a barrier and no one cared if my clients presented as unkept. No bank accounts or pay stubs were requested, neither was a letter of reference from your previous landlord. I throughly enjoyed my work as a frontline worker!

In my position as a Social Policy Developer, I have observed through the reporting process, that communities are facing a housing crisis and the demand is greater than the supply. There needs to be more purpose built housing which will ensure that there is new housing stock injected into an already saturated market.

Moving from frontline to social policy work has given me greater insight, and working on the frontline has heightened my ability to recognize the differences made in the lives of individuals; one person at a time. I miss the direct contact with homeless individuals as they move from hopelessness and homelessness to housing. It's a difficult time ahead for clients in that transition, and housing workers are making a difference.

RICHIE

Musician and Craft Specialist
Formerly Homeless

Am a proud Indigenous Quebecor. Richie is the name.

I felt important to share my experience post being housed and being counselled by several workers. I sat in this same spot waiting for my habitually late worker. She always seemed to be in a streetcar that ran late, but who really cared. Every worker says the TTC was late when they are running behind for their appointment. I needed her support to get out of the hell hole I called home. Although I had a hard time with her style of work, I kept it to myself sometimes. I needed to be housed and she seemed to have a relentless spirit.

After seven minutes walking towards my former home, I decided to prepare her for entering my apartment. I had met her at the community Drop In and knew she had no tolerance for slum landlords. Her no nonsense manner was both good and bad; today I wanted none of the above, silence was my preference. I reminded her that despite the floors being of mud and lacking much, it was much better than what my reserve had to offer. Of course she interrupted me with her usual social work banter. "Did you use the food bank, did you pay your rent and did you make your appointment to see your income support worker?" Her questions were never ending.

I reminded her food banks were for lazy people who use drugs and waste their money weekly. I cannot fathom these people who cost my Gov't money. Of course I was not allowed to say this and she did not hesitate to state she works from "a non judgemental, anti- oppressive framework, and it's a stereotype many have regarding low income individuals who are marginalized by addictions, mental health and poverty. You are those people too Richie; you are marginalized by ethnicity, unemployment and poverty" and all the social work language she learned in school. I came to Toronto because my reserve had lots of problems and I wanted a better life. If I was not displaced by government policies and bureaucracy, I would remain there. The government is paying all sorts of agencies to help Indigenous communities, so you are not doing me a favour. Looking back, I think this was the first of many battles I would have with my worker Sian, who would end the meeting for my oppressive language.

It was her right to take a stand and it was mines to share my experience with her.

Besides as mentioned before, I loved the place and the landlord was great, but the unit did not have a floor and she was best suited to help me get out and find a more habitable place. I am well aware it was better than my reserve which lacked adequate heat.

Upon visiting the unit, Sian became alarmed when she saw no plumbing in the kitchen and bathroom sink. I gently asked her to be quiet, given the landlord lived upstairs. In the three months since being here, I felt warmth and secure, given the police station was just across the street. This was important to me because, if ever I needed something, I would go to them first.

You guessed it, Sian lost her mind with the state of the unit and blurted out "This basement is an illegal rental, no one should ever have to live in a unit that has no running water and a dirt floor. I suggest you stop paying rent for this place. This is not even a unit. This is a dug out basement. You need to leave here ASAP."

So easy for her to say I opined. She never had to live on a reserve where your family are all addicts, not to mention she has never been to jail for the last 17 years of your life and know what it means to be in a place that you have control. I guess she did not. She thought my life story is one for the history books that my foremothers did not write. What gives her the right to talk about what I need or that of my community. She just did not have a clue!

Again, this session was one of many that did not end well. I was trying hard to not let my anger and past trauma impact my working relationship with my worker, but it continued and somehow I felt trapped in my own world of being failed by the system.

Before she could explain the process of the new housing she had found for me, I said, "Fine nigger whatever. No one helps anyways." In disbelief she said *"Excuse me, our meeting would end today because I cannot emphasize to you that verbal abuse is not part of my pay cheque. The next time we meet, I would like us to go to the library to read about oppressive language and behavior."*

You know me, I said. Listen, I am not racist, so there is no need. It's just a figure of speech, but that's who she was anyway.

It took about three weeks for me to see her again and she was so formal, I thought I was in some office getting an interview or something. She provided me with all the details of the housing she had found as per my sole request and took me to view the unit. I accepted and signed the lease the same day. Between the money from social assistance, my Band, selling my crafts and playing music at the subway, I was certain I had enough money for the rent. My rent was based on rent geared to income which amounted to $115. A steal I would say.

I owed Sian an apology but I never offered one.

She took me to the library and I listened to what she shared about her own community experience with colonialism. She had surely earned my respect, given for the first time in ten plus years, I had the opportunity to be adequately housed and as she would say, having access to safe and affordable housing.

Our meeting ended with Sian congratulating me on my new housing and her formally discharging me from being her client. She redirected me to Indigenous services in my neighbourhood and a community health centre.

While out and about in the community, I have seen

Sian once, but I did not acknowledge her and I think it's best that way. Wish I had said thanks to her or update her on how much my life has improved since being housed six years ago through her efforts.

VLAD

Harm Reduction Worker

Sharing my experience is not necessarily an easy one for me. I have lost friends to the opioid crisis and I have seen clients die at my location of work. I started my work at Local Community Initiatives and then moved to 'Shelter Stay'. This program is a flagship program in the City of Toronto. My role requires me to provide hands on harm reduction tools and skills to individuals struggling with substance abuse. For some, their substance of choice is illegal; not regulated, and the risk of overdosing is higher.

While for others it's prescription or 'over the counter' pain relievers. The hardest challenge for me in recent months has been the administration of Naloxone.

Naloxone reverses the effects of opioids, including extreme drowsiness, slowed breathing, or loss of consciousness. As an outreach worker doing the evening shifts, I use about 12-15 kits a week. I am broken by the pressure to save lives and burden. If the clients don't survive it's hard.

This work has changed me.

My emotions are gone.

No one told me that my resume would one day have a BSW in Traumatic Events and Complexed Stories.

I function as a wall.

I've lost so many clients that I've stopped counting.

Short term disability is not enough.

My supervisor is so detached from the work.

He never worked a day on the frontline.

He proudly boasts of all the funding he has secured from City Hall.

Look at my arms...

These are scars from me harming myself.

At times, I think if I bleed, the pain would one day subside.

I AM frontline.

In Solidarity
Break your silence

Join the conversation with frontline workers to discuss topics of support, vicarious trauma, grief and loss in the workplace and other coping strategies.

9 781927 020012